Kindergarten with Charlie

Dedicated to my brother Rashid

by T. J. Jérémie
Illustrated by Yvon Augustin

It was Corey's first day of kindergarten. He had a shiny, new red lunch box and a new blue backpack with an alligator on it. He felt happy to start his first day at school..
Inside of his backpack, his mother put a pack of crayons,
a coloring book, two pencils, and his favorite stuffed bear.

"If you feel sad, or if you miss your daddy and me." said Corey's mom,
"you can ask your teacher if you can hold Charlie"

Charlie was Corey's stuffed bear. Corey had loved Charlie ever since he was a little baby. His initials were sewn onto Charlie's right paw: C-D-S, for Corey David Shelton.

Corey and Charlie were always together. They sat next to each other in the back seat of Mommy and Daddy's car, they went to the playground together to play, and Charlie even joined Corey on every bike ride.

Today Charlie was joining Corey on his first day of kindergarten.

They were happy.

Corey sat alone on the school bus. He didn't really like the bus because the ride felt too bumpy. It smelled funny to him, and everything seemed so loud.

Corey unzipped his backpack to check on his friend. He already missed his parents.

"Are you Ok in there, Charlie?"
he asked. Corey wasn't sure he wanted to be in kindergarten anymore.

The school bus stopped. A smiling girl waved good-bye to her mother and climbed onto the school bus, holding a blue stuffed bunny. She sat down next to Corey.

"Hi, my name is Amy," the girl said. "What's your name?"

Corey looked down at his backpack. "Corey," he answered shyly.

"Do you know who your new teacher is going to be?"
Amy asked.

"I think her name is Mrs. Walsh," Corey said.

"She's my teacher too!" Amy said. "You can sit next to me at circle time!
I hope Mrs. Walsh smells good like my preschool teacher, Miss Anna."

Amy showed Corey her stuffed bunny. "This is my bunny. Her name is Nina. She's coming to kindergarten too. My mom says Nina has to stay in my cubby and wait for me today because I'm going to be pretty busy."

Corey unzipped his backpack and took out his bear. "This is Charlie," he said. "Nice to meet you, Charlie," said Amy. "Nina says hello; She's pleased to meet both of you. We can all be friends." Corey felt better now that he and Charlie had two new friends. "Maybe I do want to be a kindergartner," Corey thought.

The school bus stopped.
"OK kiddos!" said the bus driver. "We have arrived!"
"Let's go!" Amy said as she grabbed Corey's hand. "wait!" Corey said.
He threw Charlie into his backpack and swung it over his shoulders.

Corey grabbed his shiny red lunchbox
and ran to catch up with his new friend.
He didn't notice that his bag was still open.

When they arrived in front of Mrs. Walsh's door, she was standing there greeting all of her new kindergartners. She had on pretty jewelry and a bright, colorful dress "Hello, friends! It's so nice to finally meet you. I've been waiting all summer!"

Amy stood in front of Mrs. Walsh and showed her. her bunny. "This is Nina: Nina is going to wait for me in my cubby today because I'm going to be pretty busy."

"Lovely!" chuckled Mrs. Walsh. She led Corey and Amy to their cubbies to put away their belongings. "See you later Nina!" said Amy as she put her bunny away.

Corey looked into his open backpack to say good-bye to Charlie, but he wasn't there!
Corey saw his crayons, his coloring book, and even his two pencils, but Charlie was gone.

"Where is Charlie?"
asked Corey, with a worried look on his face. "I put him in my backpack,
but now I can't find him!"

"Oh no! I'm so sorry, Corey," said Mrs. Walsh. "I can call Mr. Stein, the school custodian, and maybe he can help you find your bear after lunchtime."

Mrs. Walsh gave Corey a tight hug. "I promise to try my best to help you find your bear."

"Don't worry, Corey." said Amy "I can help you find Charlie too."
Corey wasn't feeling better. He just wanted Charlie back.

At circle time Corey was very sad.
All he could think about was his lost bear.

Where is Charlie?

During math time, Corey could not concentrate. "Is he at a farm?" he wondered.

Where is Charlie?

During reading time, he was still worried. "Could he be by a pond?" he wondered.

Where is Charlie?

During art time, Corey could still only think about his lost bear.

The children in Mrs. Walsh's class saw that Corey was sad, so they drew pictures at the end of art time to make Corey feel better. He loved the pictures, but he was still feeling sad. Corey just missed Charlie.

When it was time for lunch, Corey wasn't really hungry. His mommy made his favorite: a ham and swiss cheese sandwich with the crusts cut off.
But he was too sad to eat

Where could Charlie be?

A short, round man walked into the room with a bunch of noisy keys hanging from his pants. He was holding a dirty stuffed bear. "Is anybody missing a bear?" he said in a deep and loud voice.

"Hello, Mr. Stein!" said Mrs. Walsh. "My friend Corey lost his friend Charlie. Corey is that Charlie?"

Corey jumped up and walked over to Mr. Stein to get a closer look. He saw his initials on the bear's right paw! "That's Charlie," Corey nodded. "Those are my initials: C-D-S."

"I think... I think he fell out of my backpack because I forgot to zip it."
"Great!" Said Mrs. Walsh "Thank you Mr. Stein. You saved the day."

"Thank you." said Corey as he reached out to take his stuffed bear back.
Mrs. Walsh's kindergarten class cheered and clapped for Corey.
They were all happy that Corey had found his bear.

"No problem!" said Mr. Stein. "Remember to always zip up your backpack,
or else you could lose something very important. I'm happy you found your friend.
Welcome to kindergarten."

During circle time at the end of the day, Mrs. Walsh let Corey hold Charlie in his lap. Charlie was all dirty, but Corey did not mind. He had his bear back.

and he was happy.

Kindergarten With Charlie
Written by T. J. Jérémie   Illustrated by Yvon Augustin

Made in the USA
Middletown, DE
10 June 2019